The Gypsy Ballads OF GARCIA LORCA

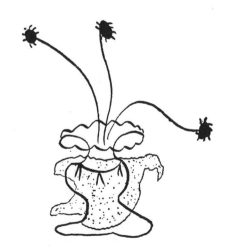

TRANSLATED BY ROLFE HUMPHRIES

WITH *3* HISTORICAL BALLADS

The Gypsy Ballads

of FEDERICO GARCÍA LORCA

Indiana University Press   BLOOMINGTON & LONDON

SIXTH PRINTING 1972

253-13670-9   cl
253-29902-X   pa

for

Nacho and Verna Millan
R.H.

Translator's Note

THESE poems are, in my considered opinion, Lorca's finest work. In translating them, and in revising translations begun over ten years ago, the things I have tried to keep are the beat of the original cadence, the strangeness of mood and atmosphere, the images, of course, and some sense, where I can, of the music. Except in one poem, the prosody is that of blank verse; I have tossed in rhymes at random, where they would not seem forced, and I have made more conscious use of assonance than one ordinarily does when composing verse in English. I hope it came out sounding something like poetry.

The thanks of the translator are due, most recently, to Samuel Yellen, editor of the Poetry Series, to Professor Glen D. Willbern of the Department of Spanish of Indiana University, and to the poet's brother, Señor Francisco García Lorca.

Rolfe Humphries

Mexico, 1938
New York, 1953

Contents

Introduction

Federico García Lorca is the most powerful of modern Spanish poets, and his *Gypsy Ballads* (*Romancero Gitano*) his most characteristic work. In these eighteen poems, with their bare, short lines, their striking images, and their colorful, changing landscape, there is Spain herself, there is a synthesis of that life, full of violence, beauty, and sorrow, of passion and gloom, which only Cervantes pictured to the full. Through the Spanish gypsy, often more Spanish than the Spanish themselves, García Lorca describes, now with dry precise detail, again with sensuous images dazzling in their impact, the existence of the hunted outcasts of Spain, in whom the soul of the land bleeds and dies and renews itself, proud but flexible, rising in its bitter humor and ancient endurance against the oppression and cruelty of centuries.

The swift movement of these poems passes through various planes of consciousness: through light and shadow, matter and spirit, fantasy and brutal reality. The poet's metaphors are most often of the senses; as he said:

A poet must be a professor of the five bodily senses, of the five senses, in the following order: sight, touch, hearing, smell, and taste. To command the most perfect images, he must open doors of communication between all of the senses. . . . The metaphor is always ruled by vision, though at times by a sublimated vision; it is the vision, too, which limits a metaphor and gives it reality. It does not permit a shadow to blur the outlines of an image it has seen clearly drawn. . . . All images are born in the visual field. . . . The metaphor links two antagonistic worlds through an equestrian leap of imagination. . . .

A poetical image is always a transference of meaning. A language consists of images, and that of our people has an immense wealth of them. . . . To call one sweetmeat "Heaven's Bacon" and another "Nun's Sigh" is to create two delightful and yet acute images; the same with the expression "Half-orange" for a cupola, and so forth. In Andalucía, popular imagery reaches astounding depths of penetration and sensitiveness, it achieves transformations much like Góngora's. Thus they call a deep watercourse that flows slowly through the fields "an ox of water," to indicate its volume and mighty, harnessed strength. And I have heard a farmer from Granada say, "The rushes love to grow on the tongue of the river." These are two images created by the people, closely corresponding to Góngora's style.

Part of this seems an echo of Rimbaud's "dérèglement de tous les sens," and there is much in Lorca's poetry which recalls symbolist doctrine; but he was too much of an individualist to be greatly influenced except in his latest period by foreign theories. The chief sources for his technique were Luis de Góngora, the old Spanish *romances,* and Andalusian folk song. The rest came from loving and accurate observation, from a keen ear for melody, and a sensitive, ever-fresh response to the life of the people he knew best.

The *Gypsy Ballads* made him famous. He never reached their level again in his creative life, which became increasingly absorbed with death; it may have been in a desperate attempt to recover that vital inspiration they breathe that he turned in his later poems to a strange surrealism, the jazz-age poems of *The Poet in New York*. The *Ballads* made his name known even to illiterate farmers and workmen; hardly anything he wrote afterwards found so strong and genuine an appeal.

The form of the *Ballads* is that of the *Cid* and the old Spanish ballads: the simple octosyllabic line with three stresses and assonance. The poet's deep preoccupation with folk songs is fundamental in his poetry; he gathered and set down the musical notation for many of them, and in a recently translated lecture on "Children's Cradle Songs" (*Zero*, 1949-50, Nos. 3-4) he wrote:

In all my walks around Spain, slightly tired of cathedrals, of dead stones, of living landscapes, I started looking for everlasting, living elements, in which the minute does not freeze, but where a shaky present lives. Among the existing infinities, I have found two: songs and sweetmeats. While a cathedral remains nailed to an epoch, giving a continuous expression of yesterday to the ever-moving landscape, a song suddenly jumps out of that yesterday into our present, lively and filled with beatings, like a frog, incorporated into the panorama like a late shrub, bringing the vivid light of old hours, thanks to the blast of the melody. . . .

In the melody, as in the sweetmeat, the emotion of history, its lasting light without dates or facts, takes refuge. The love and breeze of our country are inherent in the tunes or in the exquisite paste of the *turrón*, bringing vivid life out of dead epochs, the opposite of the stones, the bells, the people with character or even the language.

The melody, to a greater extent than the text, defines the geographical characters and the historic lineage of a region, and marks out, in an acute way, defined moments of a profile which time has rubbed out. A romance, of course, is not perfect until it carries along with it its own melody, which gives it the blood and the palpitation and the rigid or erotic atmosphere in which the characters evolve.

The horses, the gypsies, the moons, the rushing winds, the music and the fantasy of the *Ballads* are in the Spanish folk song too. There is also the sinister hint of sudden quarrels and death.

Love and death, sex and destruction are linked and fundamental themes. The dark menace of rape is grotesquely fanciful in "Preciosa and the Wind"; it is real and appalling in "The Civil Guard." Incest is the burden of "Thamar and Amnon," against the background of the hot desert. The vague fears of the girl in "Black Trouble" are also no doubt for her lover (lest he be unfaithful?) and the gypsy in "Walking Asleep," driven mad with longing for the smuggler she loves, drowns herself, like another Ophelia, in the cistern when he staggers back to die of his wounds.

Witchcraft and magic also play their part in these poems. The moon bewitches the little boy who made fun of her in "The Moon, the Moon"; Pan, identified with St. Christopher, in a Dantesque combination of pagan and Christian elements, puts to panic flight the little gypsy girl with her tambourine in "Preciosa and the Wind"; "The Man Who Was Summoned" is caught in a spell for his sins and doomed to die at a specified date; "Walking Asleep" has a Sleeping Beauty sort of trance-like quality which suggests enchantment. In the ballads about the three saints, Michael, Raphael, and Gabriel, and in "The Martyrdom of St. Eulalie" religious eroticism makes its appearance—in the visions of the torture and mutilation of the female saint; in the quaint picture of St. Michael, richly dressed in his tower while women pass and the Bishop of Manila intones a "two-edged" mass; and in Gabriel's appearance to a gypsy maid as a beautiful youth wearing patent leather shoes, the Holy Annunciation having been transposed to Seville.

The violence and tragedy of gypsy life shock the reader both in the ballads which describe their own deadly quarrels and in those which depict the murderous cruelty of the Civil Guard, for generations the peculiarly Spanish form of official repression, an army of professional bullies in three-cornered hats ready to kill, loot, and rape at a moment's notice. Like the Holy Office of Cervantes' day they patrol the roads and through them the Church, the landlords, and the military have kept the people in ignorance, poverty, and fear. They are thoroughly revealed in the ballad of "The Civil Guard"; and the hate they inspire glitters throughout the poem. It is here that Lorca uses the frightful image of a gypsy girl with her breasts cut off by the sabres of the Civil Guard, the same image he had used in "The Martyrdom of St. Eulalie," thus transposing to modern Spanish life what had been only a feature in the story of a saint. This is another hint of the mingled elements of pagan and Christian history. In the

"Fracas," where Juan Antonio of Montilla rolls down the hill after being knifed, the "four Romans dead and five Carthaginians" represent the traditional masks employed in religious processions as well as two of the peoples who have ruled Spain; they also signify two rival gypsy factions who have come to blows at the festival. "The Man Who Was Summoned" rests at last in a bed whose straight sheets have a Roman "accent"; the waves polish and turn a Roman torso, naked, in the opening lines of "San Raphael (Córdoba)." The past is always present in a European country, but perhaps nowhere more unalterably evident than in Spain, where the Roman occupation and the Middle Ages have left their imprint everywhere.

The images of Lorca's *Ballads* are famous; and yet, his theory of poetry understood, they present no real difficulty. Most of them rest upon some realistic fact of sense-perception; it is only because they are unexpected that they puzzle us. The moon's tin breasts are an apt figure, for the moon's coldness and that of tin are much the same, glittering in the night; the light hard as playing cards is another exact image, strange only because we have not thought of it as we shuffled them. The gypsy nun's heart of sugar and spice is a compact way of picturing her longing for the rider who gallops by, as it extends beyond her candy-making and weaving; the starchy skirts of the unfaithful wife crackle like sheets of silk cut by twenty shears, an exact evocation of sound. The cocks with their picks dig for the dawn as to Lorca they seemed to do; and if Solitude Montoya (whose given name is used both literally and symbolically in "Black Trouble") is told by her imaginary interlocutor (or by her inner voice) to wash her body in an extract of larks, it is only to make her as happy as a lark. The water at Cordova that makes two towns of one is a simple image: its statement is the inevitable and unerring utterance of a poet. Wind, heat, light, sound, colors, the moon and stars, the water, flowers, horses, soldiers, and gypsies

—all are part of the poet's sensation as he speaks of them again and again. His imagery has another peculiar trait—the specificity of numbers: three riflemen rush down at Preciosa's shrieks; two old women cry and four Romans and five Carthaginians die in the "Fracas"; three hundred crimson roses deck the shirt front of the wounded smuggler; seven prismatic birds thread the grey chandelier, five yellow grapefruit sweeten, in the gypsy nun's home; twenty suns shine above the plain outside; sheets of silk are cut by twenty shears and the unfaithful wife wears four lace petticoats; "your son shall have a mole and three wounds in his breast," says Saint Gabriel to the gypsy virgin, and three balls of green almond trill in his voice; five Civil Guards arrest Antoñito El Camborio, lock him up precisely at nine o'clock, and he dies one against four assailants, spurting three gouts of blood; four blazing torches shine in the heavens for the one who died of love; seven cries, bloods, and poppies smashed the opaque moons in the mirrors of dark rooms in his house; it is on August 25, just one month after he received his citation, that the summoned one lay down and died; five frozen doves lie at Thamar's feet and Amnon's hundred horses neigh in the nearby court. This numerical accuracy becomes almost an affectation, but there is no doubt that it narrows and focuses the reader's vision. For this is the function of Lorca's imagery: to focus and at the same time to extend the vision of his reader. Some may regard certain far-fetched images as fantastic; but Lorca was seeking phrases never used before to express his insights, as Góngora did before him; he sought them out first in the world of the senses and then, like a gypsy blacksmith, struck off his metaphor in a shower of sparks.

Perhaps the most remarkable characteristic of the *Gypsy Ballads* is the powerful sense of life they give forth. The moods each one creates arise from an intense feeling for the major phases of existence, love and death, which is without parallel in modern Spanish literature. For the tragic sense of life these poems reveal we must go back to Cervantes and to the half-unreal atmosphere of the Sierra Morena; we must go back to Don Quixote, that noble comrade of Spain's humble people, who like them was scorned and beaten and yet kept his sanity at the end. There is in Cervantes' novel the same panorama, the same gloomy landscape, the hard realities of mountain and plain, with the poetry always beneath—and the pathos.

Manuel de Falla, Pablo Picasso, Federico García Lorca—perhaps it is only accident that they were all born in Andalucía. These three men typify the arts Lorca practised—music and painting, as an inspired amateur, poetry, as a unique creator. The *Gypsy Ballads*, written by 1924 and published in 1928, were his first successful combination of music, color, and verse; he was never to surpass them or to return to them. Other kinds of poetry and the drama absorbed his energies until at Fuentevaqueros, the little village near Granada where he had been born on June 5, 1899, the poet was murdered by the Civil Guard in August, 1936. The order of death was signed, according to José Bergamín, by the authorities of Granada, formally representing the rebel Junta of Burgos, the *de facto* government of Francisco Franco.

L. R. Lind

The moon, the moon

The moon comes to the forge
With a bustle of nard, in style:
The child stares at the moon
Fixedly all the while.
Across the moving air
The moon holds out her arms,
Her metal breasts are bare,
Shiny and pure and hard.

"Run away, run away, Moon!
For if the gypsies come
They'll stamp your silver heart
For bangle and ring and charm."
"Stop, child, let me dance.
When the gypsies come to-night,
They'll find you on the anvil
With your little eyes shut tight."

"Run away, run away, Moon!
I hear their horses near."
"Stop, child, do not crush
My starched and shiny dress."

Rider and horse appear
With a long roll of the drum,
The great drum of the plain,
And the child's little eyes
Shut tight against the scene.

From fields of olive come
The gypsies, dreamy and brown,

The head held very high,
The sleepy eyes half-down.

How the screech-owl sends
Her long-drawn wailing cry
While the moon with the child
Wends across the sky.

And in the smithy tears,
Tears, and gypsy crying
And the wail of the watching wind,
Watching, watching, and hiding.

Preciosa and the Wind

Playing her parchment moon,
Preciosa comes along
Down an amphibian path
Of laurel and crystal glass.
The starless silence falls
Fleeing the singsong tune
Where the roaring sea intones
Its dark mysterious song
Of an ocean of fish at night.
High on the mountain peaks
Riflemen lie asleep
Guarding the towers of white
Where the English people live.
And the gypsies of the water
Build, to amuse themselves,
Arbors of white sea-shells
And branches of dark-green pine.

Playing her parchment moon,
Preciosa comes along.
The wind who never sleeps
Gets up to look at her.
Big old Christopher,
Naked, with heavenly tongues,
Looks at the girl and plays
A sweet little absent tune.
"My dear, let me lift your dress,
Let me look at you, my dear:
Let my gnarled old fingers open
Your belly's bluish rose."

Dropping her tambourine
Preciosa runs away.
Lusty and male, the wind
Pursues with his red-hot sword.

Ocean ruffles its roar
And the olive-trees turn pale,
The flutes of shadow sing
And the snow is a soothing gong.

Run, Preciosa, run,
Dont let the green wind gain!
Run, Preciosa, run,
He's coming with might and main,
Satyr of fallen stars
With gleaming, glittering tongues.

Preciosa, scared to death,
Enters the lofty house
Over the timber line
Where the English consul lives.

Startled, the riflemen come,
Three of them, at her crying,
Folded in capes of black,
Vizors over their eyes.

The Englishman gives the gypsy
A glassful of lukewarm milk
And a little cup of gin.
Preciosa does not drink.

She cries and tells these people
Her sad and dangerous tale
While the furious wind is leaping
And biting the roofs of slate.

Fracas

Halfway down the canyon
Daggers of Albacete
Bright with the blood of rivals
Glimmer and shine like fish.
Light like a deck of cards
Hard and glossy and white
Cuts in the brittle green
Horses rearing in fright,
Profiles of horses and riders.
In the bower of an olive-tree
Two old women are crying.

The great bull of the brawl
Clambers over the walls.
Sable angels bring
Kerchiefs and glacier-water.
Angels with mighty wings
Of the daggers of Albacete.
Juan Antonio's dead
Tumbling down the rocks,
His body is full of lilies,
A pomegranate in his brain,
Riding a fiery cross
Along the highway of death.

The judge and the Civil Guard
Come through the olive grove.
The slippery blood gives tongue,
A dumb and snaky song.
"Gentlemen, here we have
The same old story again:

Romans, four of them dead;
Carthaginians, five."

The afternoon gone mad
With fig-trees and burning rumors
Falls fainting in a swoon
On the wounded thighs of the riders.
And angels of black go flying
To the far air of the West,
Angels with hearts of oil
And long and braided tress.

Walking asleep

Green as I would have you be.
Green wind. Green boughs.
The boat on the sea
And the horse on the mountain.
With shadow around her waist
She is dreaming at her railing,
Green flesh, green hair,
Eyes of frozen silver.
Green as I would have you be.
Under the gypsy moon,
Things are watching her,
Things she cannot see.

Green as I would have you be.
Great stars of hoar-frost
Come with the shadowy fish
That opens the road of dawn.
The fig-tree rubs the wind
On its abrasive boughs;
The mountain, catamount,
Thrusts out her sharpened thorns.
Who's coming? By what road?
She lingers at her railing,
Green flesh, green hair,
Dreams of the bitter sea.

"Old man, I'd like to change
My pony for your house,
My saddle for your mirror,
My dagger for your blanket.

Old man, I come bleeding
From Cabra's mountain passes."

"If I could, my lad,
We might strike a bargain,
But I hardly know who I am,
Nor is my house my own."

"Old man, I'd like to die
Decently in my bed
Of steel, if that could be,
Between the linen sheets.
My wound,—or dont you see?—
Reaches from chest to throat."

"Three hundred crimson roses
Stain your white shirt red;
The blood smells and oozes
Around the swathing bands.
But I hardly know who I am,
Nor is my house my own."

"Let me climb at least
To the high railing;
Let me climb, I pray,
To the green railing,
The moon's balustrade
By the sounding water."

Now they both are climbing
To the high railing,
Leaving a bloody trail,
Leaving a trail of tears.
Little tinny lights

Wink across the roof-tops:
A thousand crystal timbrels
Wound the early dawn.

Green as I would have you be.
Green wind. Green boughs.
Both of them are climbing.
The wind leaves in the mouth
A rare and generous savor,
Gall and mint and basil.
"Old man! Where is she, tell me,
Tell me where she is,
That bitter girl, your daughter?"
"How long she waited for you!
How long, how vainly leaning,
Bright face, dark hair,
At this green railing!"

Over the cistern's face
Sways the gypsy lass.
Green flesh, green hair,
Eyes of frozen silver.
An icicle of moonlight
Holds her over the water.
Night becomes familiar,
A homely little plaza.
Drunken Civil Guards
Hammer on the door.

Green as I would have you be.
Green wind. Green boughs.
The boat on the sea,
And the horse on the mountain.

The gypsy nun

Myrtle and lime are still.
Mallows among the reeds.
The nun weaves gillyflowers
On straw-colored cloth.
Seven prismatic birds
Thread the gray chandelier.
Far off, the church is growling
Like a bear, belly up.
How prettily embroidered,
How gracefully and fine!
On straw-colored cloth
She wanted to be weaving
Imaginary flowers.
Spangle and ribbon make
Magnolia and sunflower,
Such saffron, and such moonflower
Upon the altar-cloth.
Within the nearby kitchen
Five yellow grapefruit sweeten,
The five wounds of Christ
Cut in Almería.
Across the eyes of the nun
Two loping riders move.
A dull and distant murmur
Loosens her white apparel,
And seeing clouds and mountain
In distances unyielding,
Her heart of herbs and sugar,
Of spice and sweet, is broken.
O far-extending plain

With twenty suns above!
O streams on tiptoe poised
By glimmering fancy seen!
But she stays with her flowers
While above in the breeze
The light keeps playing chess
Over the jalousies.

The unfaithful married woman

I took her to the river,
Believing her unwed;
The fact she had a husband
Was something left unsaid.
St. James's night is timely—
She would not let me wait—
The lights are put out early,
The fireflies light up late.

I roused her sleeping bosom
Right early in our walk;
Her heart unfolded for me
Like hyacinths on the stalk.
Her starchy skirts kept rustling
And crackled in my ears
Like sheets of silk cut crosswise
At once by twenty shears.

The dark unsilvered treetops
Grew tall, as on we strode;
Dogs barked, a whole horizon,
Far from the river road.

When we had passed the brambles
And the thickets on our round,
Her coiled hair made a pillow
In a hollow on the ground:
As I undid my necktie,
Her petticoats left their place;
I shed my leather holster,
And she, four layers of lace.

Not nard nor snail had ever
Texture of skin so fine,
Nor crystal in the moonlight
Glimmered with purer shine:
Her thighs slipped from beneath me
Like little trout in fright,
Half chilly (but not frigid),
Half full of shining light.

The whole night saw me posting
Upon my lovely mare;
Mother-of-pearl the saddle,
No need for bridle and spur;
And what her whispers told me
A man should not repeat
When perfect understanding
Has made the mind discreet.

Dirty with sand and kisses
I brought her from the shore
As the iris poised green sabres
At the night wind once more.

To act in decent fashion
As loyal gypsy should,
I gave her a sewing-basket,
Satin and straw, and good;
And yet I would not love her
In spite of what she said
When I took her to the river,
For she was not unwed.

Black trouble

The cocks with their picks
Dig for the dawn;
Down the dark mountain
Solitude comes.
Yellow copper, her flesh
Smells of horses and dusk;
Smoky anvils, her breasts
Moan circular songs.

"Whom are you seeking
Alone at this hour?"
"Never mind whom I seek,
What is it to you?
I seek what I seek,
My joy and myself."

"Solitude of my sorrows,
The horse with hard mouth
Ends up in the sea
And is swallowed by waves."
"Dont talk of the sea
With black trouble flooding
In the rustle of leaves
Through the lands of the olive."

"What trouble is yours,
What terrible trouble!
You weep lemon juice,
Bitter-mouthed from the waiting."

Terrible trouble!
I run through the house
Braids to the ground
As a mad woman ranges
Kitchen to chamber.
Terrible trouble
Turning jet-black
Body and clothing,
Shirts that were linen,
Thighs that were poppies."

"Solitude, bathe
In an extract of larks,
Let the heart be at peace,
Solitude of the mountains."

Below sings the river,
A flounce of the sky,
With an imprint of leaves:
The new light is crowned
With the flowers of the gourd.
O gypsy trouble,
Pure and alone,
Always alone
The secret channel,
The far-off dawn!

Saint Michael (Granada)

Visible from the railing
Mules and shadows of mules
Laden with sunflowers come
Up the mountain, mountain, mountain.

Their eyes in the shadows fill,
Darken, with deepest night.
In the wind's angles
A brackish dawn crackles.

A sky of mules of white
Closes quicksilver eyes,
Giving the quiet dawn
Affectionate farewell:
Water, crazy, unloosed
Turns too cold for the touch
On the mountain, mountain, mountain.

St. Michael, rich in lace,
In the alcove of his tower,
Shows his beautiful thighs
Ringed in the lanterns' light.

Archangel, tame, drawn up,
In the pose of the hands at noon,
Feigns benevolent wrath
Soft as nightingale down.

St. Michael sings at the window.
A youth of three thousand nights,
Fragrant with eau-de-cologne,
Far from the scent of the flower.

The dance of the sea on the shore
Is a balcony kind of poem;
The margins of the moon
Lose reed and rush, gain voice.
Common wenches come
Nibbling sunflower seeds,
Their bottoms hidden and big
Half-moons of coppery plate.
Lofty lords appear,
Ladies of doleful mien,
Brown with nostalgia, yearn
For nightingale yesterdays.
And the Bishop of Manila,
Blind with saffron, and poor,
Intones a two-edged mass,
For women and for men.

St. Michael was very still
In the alcove of his tower,
His vestments frozen stiff
With spangles interwoven.

St. Michael, king of spheres,
And of odd numbers king,
Perfect in Berber grace
Of cry and oriel.

Saint Raphael (Córdoba)

I

Closed coaches were coming
To the edge of the rushes
Where the waves polish and turn
A Roman torso, naked.
Coaches that Guadalquivir
Holds in her glassy ripeness
Between the gloss of the flower
And the double depth of the cloud.
Shuttling children sing
The naked truth of the world
Around the coaches, old
And lost in the dark of night.
And Cordova never wavers
In that mysterious dark,
For if the shadow lifts
The structure of its smoke
A marble foot discloses
Austere and luminous white,
While petals made of tin
Plate the purest grays
Of a wind, a breeze unfurled
Over triumphal arches;
And while the bridge whispers
Ten rumors of King Neptune,
Tobacco sellers flee
Along the broken wall.

11

One fish alone in the water
That makes two towns of one:
Soft Cordova of rushes,
And Cordova of stone.
Children with no expression
Undress among the rushes,
Disciples of Tobias,
Slender-waisted Merlins
Who plague the single fish
With this ironic riddle,
"Does he want flowers of wine,
Or half-moon waterfalls?"
But the fish, who gilds the water
And makes the marble mournful,
Gives them a lesson in poise,
A solitary column.
Archangel, a trifle Moorish,
Dressed in dark spangles, seeking
Where the waves held their meeting
For rumor and for cradle.

One fish alone in the water:
Two Cordovas of beauty.
One broken in spurts of water,
One dry in the high heaven.

Saint Gabriel (Seville)

I

Beautiful youth of reed,
Wide shoulders, narrow waist,
Skin of an apple at night,
Sad mouth, enormous eyes,
With nerves of burning silver,
Patrols the narrow street.
His patent-leather shoes
Sprout dahlias on the air,
And sing in antiphon
Of brief celestial grief.

Along the seashore stands
No palm as tall as he,
No lofty emperor crowned,
Nor moving morning star,
And when his head is bowed
Upon his jasper breast
The night seeks level plains
Whereon to bend the knee.
Guitars alone resound
Archangel Gabriel!
Tamer of little doves
And foe of willow-trees.
"Gabriel, the child weeps
Within the mother's womb.
Do not forget, the gypsies
Gave you the suit you wear."

II

Regal Annunciation,
Ill-clad, in moonlight shining,
Welcomes the morning star
That comes along the street,
Archangel Gabriel,
Grandson of La Giralda,
Halfway between a smile
And the lilies of the field,
Comes down to visit her.
In his embroidered jacket
The hidden crickets tick;
The stars of the night
Turn to little bells.

"Lord Gabriel, here am I
With three nails of gladness:
Your brilliance scatters jasmines
Over my glowing face."

"God bless you, Annunciation,
Wonderful dusky flower,
For you shall bear a son
Fairer than stalks of the wind."

"Gabriel, lord of wonder,
Dear little saint of my life,
Out of my dreams I fashion
An arm-chair for you to rest in
Of the tiniest carnations."

"God bless you, Annunciation,
Ill-clad, in moonlight shining!

Your son shall have a mole
And three wounds in his breast."

"Ah, Gabriel, shining saint,
Dear little saint of my life,
Deep in my breasts I feel
The warm milk come to birth."

"God bless you, Annunciation,
Mother of kings on kings!
Your eyes are dry and burning,
Like plains the horsemen know."

The child sings in the womb,
As Annunciation marvels.
Three green-almond balls
Trill in his little voice.
St. Gabriel ascends
The stairway of the air;
The stars of the night
Turn to immortelles.

Arrest of little Tony Camborio, on the Seville Road

Antonio Torres Heredia,
Camborios' son and grandson,
Goes with a wand of willow
To see the bulls at Seville.
Brown in the green of the moonlight,
Elegant, strolling slowly,
With blue bangs, curled and oily,
Shining between his eyes.
Halfway down the highway
He starts to cut round lemons
Throwing them in the water
Until it turns to gold,
And halfway down the highway,
Under the boughs of an elm-tree,
The Civil Guard, patrolling,
Truss him and march him away.

The day goes very slowly,
Afternoon swung from a shoulder,
Sweeping a bullfighter's cape
In a showy gesture over
Stream and sea and river,
The olive trees await
The night of Capricorn
And a little breeze, on horseback,
Leaps the mountains of lead.

Antonio Torres Heredia,
Camborios' son and grandson,

Goes without wand of willow
With five of the Civil Guard
Wearing three-cornered hats.

— Antonio, who are you?
Your name is not Camborio;
A real one would have made
A fountain of blood, a fountain
Whose five jets leaped and spurted.
Nobody was your father,
No real Camborio, surely.
All gone, the gypsy wanderers,
Lonely over the mountains,
And the little knives are chilly
Shivering under the dust.

At nine o'clock at night
They take him to the jail
And all the Civil Guards
Have a drink of lemonade.
At nine o'clock at night
They lock him in the jail
 And the sky has a bright shine on it
Like the crupper of a foal.

Death of little Tony Camborio

Voices of death resounding
Around the Guadalquivir,
Old voices closing around
The voice of the male carnation.
He slashed at the tops of their boots
With the tusks of a fighting boar,
He leaped in the thick of the struggle
Like a dolphin in soapy water,
He dyed his necktie crimson
With the stain of enemy blood,
But there were four knives against him
And so he had to go down.
When the stars were thrusting lances
Into the gray of the water,
And two-year-old bulls were dreaming
Cape-figures of gillyflowers,
Voices of death were sounding
Around the Guadalquivir.

— Antonio Torres Heredia,
Tough-maned Camborio warrior,
Brown in the green of the moonlight,
With the voice of the male carnation,
Who took your life away
Along the Guadalquivir?
— My four Heredia cousins,
Sons of Benamejí,
Envied nothing in others,
But they envied it in me.
Shoes the color of cherries,
Ivory medallions,

And the complexion blended
Of olive and of jasmin.
— Poor little Tony, worthy
Of a great queen or empress,
Remember the Virgin Mary
In the hour of your death!
— Ay, Federico García,
Summon the Civil Guard!
They have broken me in half
The way they break a cornstalk.

He shed three bursts of blood
In the profile of his dying.
The living coin would never
Be minted ever again.
A proud, officious angel
Placed his head on a pillow.
Four others, with faded blushes,
Lighted a candle for him.
And when his four first-cousins
Came home to Benamejí,
Voices of death were silent
Around the Guadalquivir.

Dead of love

"What's this, that shines
In the high hallways?"
"Close the door, my son:
Eleven has struck."
"In my eyes, all unwilling,
Four lanterns are shining."
"Those people again
Must be scouring the copper."

Leek of lean silver,
The moon on the wane
Sets yellowish streamers
On yellow towers.
Night calls a-tremble
At balcony windows:
Hounds by the thousands
Unknowing, pursue her.
Wine-smell and amber
Drift down the hallways.

Breeze from wet cane,
Murmur of voices,
Old phrases spoken
Under the broken
Archway of midnight.
Bullocks and roses
Are taking their slumber.
High in the hallways
Cry the four lamps
With the rage of St. George.
Sad valley women

With masculine blood,
Cool as young flower,
Sharp as young thigh,
Old river crones
At the foot of the mountain
Weep for a moment
That all is a tangle,
Of names and long hair.
Façades of lime
Whiten and square
The print of the night.
Seraphim, gypsies,
Play the accordion.
"When I die, Mother,
Tell the whole world.
Send the blue cables
Northward and Southward."

Seven cries, seven wounds,
Seven big double poppies,
Cast opaque moons
In the big dark rooms.

Full of cut hands
And chaplets of flowers,
The ocean of vows
Sounded, resounded,
Who would know where?
And the sky slammed its doors
On the brawl of the forest,
And the lights cried on
In the high hallways.

The man who was summoned

My restless solitude!
My body's little eyes,
The big eyes of my horse,
Are open all night long.
They never turn and see
A dream of thirteen boats
In peace, far out at sea,
But clean and hard and bright,
The shields of watchful squires
Fix on a stony north
Of stiff metallic rock
Where my body with no veins
Keeps looking for advice
In frozen decks of cards.

Thick oxen of the water
Charge at the boys who bathe
Between those crescent moons,
The undulating horns.
The forge walks in its sleep,
Hammer and anvil sing
The wakefulness of horse,
The wakefulness of rider.

On the twenty-fifth of June
They told The Bitter One,
"If so you please, cut down
The oleander-tree
That blossoms in the court.
Paint a cross on the door
And put your name below it:

Hemlock and nettle soon
Will settle in your side
And needles of wet lime
Will eat your shoes away.
And when the night is dark
Across magnetic hills
And water-bullocks drink
Drowsy among the rushes,
Ask for bell and candle
And learn to fold your hands,
Taste, in the chilly air,
The stiff metallic rock,
Because, within two months,
The shroud will be your garment."

St. James swung in the air
His blade of cloud and mist:
Over his shoulder leaning
The vaulted heaven sent
Its heavy silence down.

On June the twenty-fifth
The Bitter One opened his eyes;
On August the twenty-fifth,
He closed them, lying down.
Men came through the town
To see the summoned man
Who fastened to the wall
His rested solitude.
The pure and stainless sheet,
With Roman accent, gave
Its straight emphatic folds,
A balance to the grave.

The Spanish Civil Guard

Black are the black-shod horses.
Stains of ink and of beeswax
Gleam on the capes of the men.
Their deadly faces are leaden,
Therefore they never weep:
Hearts of patent-leather,
They come along the road.
Twisted, crooked, nocturnal,
They sow in the places they haunt
Sombre elastic silence,
Fears that trickle like sand.
They pass if they want to pass.
They hide in their muddled heads
An astronomical system,
Pistols for planets and stars.

O city of the gypsies!
Flags at the alley-corners,
Cherry-preserve in jars,
Pumpkins and orange and moon,
O city of the gypsies,
Who that has seen can forget?
City of musk and sorrow,
City of cinnamon towers.
And at the loom of nightfall,
Night that will nighten the night,
Gypsies over their forges
Striking out arrows and suns.
Wounded, a single stallion
Knocking at all of the doors.
Roosters of glass were crowing

By Jerez de la Frontera,
The naked wind comes around
A corner, caught by surprise
In the platinum-silver of dusk,
Night that will nighten the night.

St. Joseph and Mary the Virgin
Have lost their castanets
And start to look for the gypsies
To see if they know where they are.
The Virgin is formally dressed
Like the wife of a small-town mayor
In tinsel chocolate-wrapping,
Wearing a necklace of almonds,
St. Joseph swinging his arms
Under a silken mantle.
Behind comes Pedro Domecq,
Three Persian sultans attending,
And the half-moon in a daze
Dreams like a stork bemused.
Banners and torches gleam
Bright in their raid on the roofs.
Dancing girls, slenderly made,
Sob as they look in the glass.
Water and shadow, shadow and water
By Jerez de la Frontera.

O city of the gypsies,
Flags at the alley-corners,
Extinguish your greenish lights,
The Service is on its way!
O city of the gypsies,
Who that has seen can forget?

Leave her far from the sea,
Let down the uncombed hair.

In the city of holiday mirth
They penetrate, two by two,
A murmur of immortelles
Raiding the bandoliers.
They penetrate two by two,
A double nocturne of cloth.
The sky, in the eyes of their craving,
Looks like a showcase of spurs.

Empty from fear, the city
Doubles its number of doors:
Forty Civil Guardsmen
Promptly enter and loot.
Not to arouse suspicion
Clocks stop; cognac in flasks
Turns to November mist.
Weathervanes screech as they whirl.
Sabres slash at the breeze
Trodden by ringing hoofs.

Through the shadowy streets
The gypsy old women flee
Dragging their sleepy nags,
Clutching their money crocks.
Up the slope of the streets
Climb the sinister capes
Leaving behind the quick
Fugitive click of shears.

At the portal called Bethlehem
The gypsies gather together.

St. Joseph, covered with wounds,
Veils a young girl with a shroud.
Sharp and determined, the rifles
Clatter the whole night long.
The Virgin tends to the children
With frothy spittle of star.
Forward, the Civil Guard!
Fierce on the innocent sight
The braziers flame as they go
Setting on sudden fire
Fancy, naked and young.
Rosa de los Camborios
Sobs on the step of her door
With both breasts cut away
And placed on a serving-tray.
Other girls run, pursued
By their own long streaming hair.
Roses, powdery black,
Burst into bloom in the air.
When all the tiled roofs have come down,
Down on the ground like furrows,
Dawn with a profile of stone
Wearily rises again.

O city of the gypsies!
Flames encircle the town;
Through a tunnel of silence
The Civil Guard departs.

O city of the gypsies,
Who that has seen can forget?
Let them hold their search in my brain.
Their game of sand and moon.

Three Historical Ballads

The martyrdom of Saint Eulalie

I. General View of Mérida

A stallion with flowing tail
Gallops and rears in the street,
And Rome's old soldiers play
At dice, or lie and doze.
Minerva's mountain slope
Opens its leafless arms.
Water, poised in mid-air,
Gilds the grain in the rock.
A night of torsos a-sprawl,
Of stars with broken noses,
Waits for the cleft of dawn
To sink and crumble down.
Red-crested blasphemies
From time to time resound.
At the cry the holy girl
Breaks the goblets of glass.
The wheel whets the edge of the knife
And the gaff with its cutting spur.
The bull of the anvil roars
And Mérida is crowned
With spikenard, nearly awake,
And brambleberry thorn.

II. The Martyrdom

Flora, naked, ascends
The little stairs of water.
The consul looks for a platter
To carry Eulalie's breasts.
Arterial sprouts of green
Shoot from the shaft of the throat.

Her sex, entangled, trembles
Like a little bird in a bush.
On the ground, their pattern broken
Flutter the severed hands,
Still crossed in the little prayer,
Beheaded orisons!
Deep in the pits of red
That used to be her breasts
Diminished skies are seen
And streams of whitish milk.
A thousand little trees
Of blood conceal her shoulders,
With soaking trunks opposing
The cautery of fire.
Sallow centurions
With grizzled, watchful flesh,
Raise to the sky their silver,
Their ringing armament;
And while confusion shakes
Its rage of crest and sword,
The consul brings, on a platter,
Eulalie's smoking breasts.

III. Hell and Glory

The drifted snow reposes.
Eulalie hangs from the tree.
Her charcoal nakedness
Smudges the frozen winds.
Night glows with its own tension,
Eulalie hangs on the tree.
The inkwells of the cities
Pour out their thickness, slowly.
Manikins, dressed in black,
Cover the fields of snow

In lengthy lines bewailing
The mutilated silence.
The broken snow resumes.
Eulalie pales on the tree,
And squads of nickel fix
Their wet beaks in her side.

A single Monstrance shines
Over the burnt-out skies
Between the gorge of the stream
And nightingales on high.
The stained-glass panes are broken,
Eulalie pales in space.
Angels and seraphim
Say Holy, Holy, Holy!

Down a trail
Came Don Pedro,
Weeping and weeping.
His horse was lively
And had no bridle.
The rider wanted
Bread and kisses;
All the windows
Question the wind
Through the dark plaint
Of the cavalier.

(Words stay
Under the water;
Over the water
A round moon bathes;
High in the sky
The other one envies.
A child at the bank,
Seeing them, says,
"Night, play your cymbals!")

Don Pedro has come
To a far-off town,
A far-off town
In a cedar grove.
Bethlehem?—air
Of sage and rue.
Rooftops and clouds

Glimmer. He goes
Past arches, broken.
Two aged women
And one old man
With lamps of silver
Go out to meet him.
No! say the poplars,
And the nightingale says
We shall see, we shall see.

    (Words stay
    Under the water.
    Over the crest of the water
    A ring of birds and of flame.
    In the reeds and the sedge
    Witnesses know what is missing.
    A dream without any north,
    Hard as guitar's dark wood.)

Over the flat highway
Two women and one old man
Carrying silver lamps
To the graveyard wend their way.
In the saffron there they find
Don Pedro's black horse dead.
The afternoon's secret voice,
Plaintive, whines to the sky.
Absence, a unicorn,
Shatters his crystal horn.
The far-off town is on fire
And a man goes weeping by.
Look to the north for a star,
South, for a mariner.

(Words stay
Under the water.
Marsh and bog,
Voices lost.
Over the flower,
The blossom frozen,
Don Pedro, forgotten,
Plays with the frogs.)

Thamar and Amnon

The moon turns in the sky
Over the waterless lands,
While the summertime sows
Rumors of tiger and flame.
Over the tops of the roof
Fibers of metal rang.
The wind was crinkled and came
Woolly with bleatings of cloud.
The tissue of earth was scarred
By wounds healed over, or stung
By the cautery of white lights.

Thamar was dreaming,
Birds in her throat,
Sound of cold timbrel,
Zither's round moon.
On the top of the roof
Due north of the palm-tree,
Her nakedness wanted
Snowflake for belly,
Hail for the shoulder.
Naked again,
Down on the terrace,
Thamar was singing,
Five frozen doves
White at her feet.

High in the tower
Amnon was watching,
Slender and hard,
Groin almost foaming,

Beard all a-tremble.
Flooded with light,
His nakedness stood
Taut on the terrace,
With rumor suppressed
Of an arrow, new-fired,
That clove to the mark.
Amnon was watching
The round low moon
And he saw in the moon
The breasts of his sister,
Shiny and hard.

At half past three by the clock
Amnon lay on his bed.
The chamber suffered and shook
With the rage of his winged eyes.
The light, compact, interred
Towns in the tawny sand,
Or moving over them, stirred
Coral of dahlia and rose.
Water drawn from the wells
Made silence gush from the jars.
In the moss in the crotch of the trees
The vibrant cobra sang.

Amnon was lying alone,
Amnon was crying aloud.
At the cool touch of the sheet
Ivy of chills and fever
Shaded his burning flesh.
Thamar entered the room,
Brown as the Danube River,

Sallow with far-off roads.
Thamar entered the room,
And the room was very still.

"Thamar, darken my eyes
With your everlasting dawn.
My restless arteries weave
Flounces over your dress."
"Brother, let me alone:
Your kisses burn on my shoulder
Like the sting of wasp and the wind
In the flutes' double swarm."
"Thamar, in your high breasts
Two fish invite my hands;
The buds of your finger-tips
Hint of the buried rose."

The king's hundred horses
Neigh in the court near-by;
The bulky blocky sun
Fights through the trellised vine.
He catches her by the hair,
He rips her out of the blouse,
Coral paints on the map
Rivulets warm and red.

What cry, what cry is that?
Hearken! The house-tops hear.
The thick of the dagger-thrust,
The loosening of the dress.
Slaves go up and down
The melancholy stairs.
Thighs and pistons plunge

Under the sluggish cloud.
Gypsy virgins cry
At Thamar's side, aloud,
Or gather up the gouts
Shed by her martyred flower.
All white clothes turn red
Behind the bolted doors.
The leaves and the fish exchange
Rumors of warm dawn.

Ravager in rage,
Amnon mounts and rides.
Negroes on the wall
From parapet and tower
Loose arrows at his flight.
When the four loud hoofs
Were four echoes only,
David with his shears
Cut the harpstrings through.

Garc:

    The gypsy ballads; translated by Rolfe Humphries, with 3 historical ballads.   Bloomington Indiana University Press, 1953.

    64p. 24cm. (Indiana University poetry series)

I.Title. II.Series.